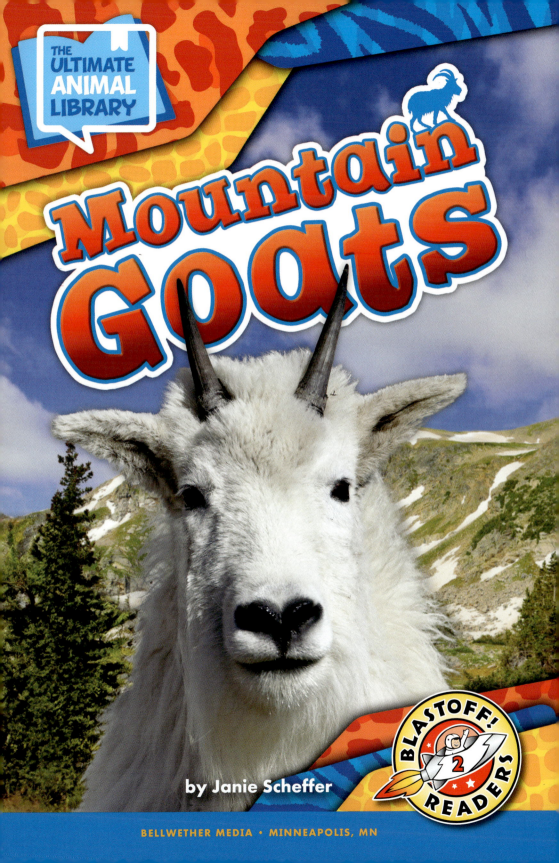

THE ULTIMATE ANIMAL LIBRARY

Mountain Goats

by Janie Scheffer

BELLWETHER MEDIA • MINNEAPOLIS, MN

Blastoff! Readers are carefully developed by literacy experts to build reading stamina and move students toward fluency by combining standards-based content with developmentally appropriate text.

Level 1 provides the most support through repetition of high-frequency words, light text, predictable sentence patterns, and strong visual support.

Level 2 offers early readers a bit more challenge through varied sentences, increased text load, and text-supportive special features.

Level 3 advances early-fluent readers toward fluency through increased text load, less reliance on photos, advancing concepts, longer sentences, and more complex special features.

★ **Blastoff! Universe**

Reading Level

Grade K

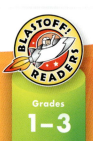
Grades 1–3

Grade 4

This edition first published in 2026 by Bellwether Media, Inc.

No part of this publication may be reproduced in whole or in part without written permission of the publisher. For information regarding permission, write to Bellwether Media, Inc., Attention: Permissions Department, 3500 American Blvd W, Suite 150, Bloomington, MN 55431.

Library of Congress Cataloging-in-Publication Data

LC record for Mountain Goats available at: https://lccn.loc.gov/2025003956

Text copyright © 2026 by Bellwether Media, Inc. BLASTOFF! READERS and associated logos are trademarks and/or registered trademarks of Bellwether Media, Inc. Bellwether Media is a division of FlutterBee Education Group.

Editor: Elizabeth Neuenfeldt   Series Designer: Veah Demmin

Printed in the United States of America, North Mankato, MN.

Table of Contents

What Are Mountain Goats? 4
Strong Climbers! 12
Growing Up 18
Glossary 22
To Learn More 23
Index 24

What Are Mountain Goats?

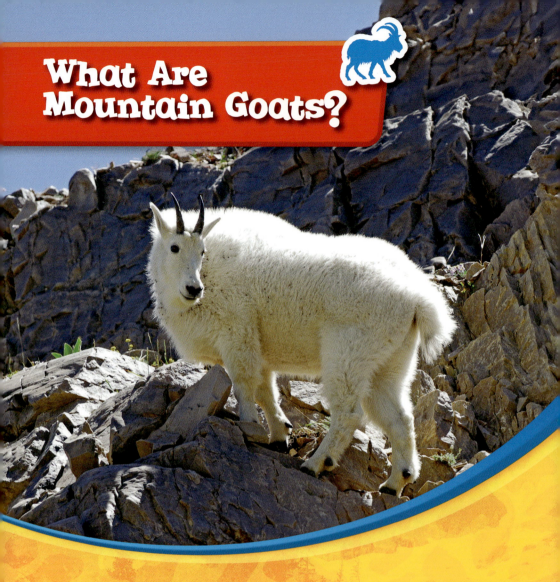

Mountain goats are **mammals**. They are known to climb high **cliffs**. They live in parts of North America.

Mountain Goat Report

Mountain goats have **shaggy**, white **coats**. Their coats are longer in winter. This keeps the goats warm.

← coat

Their coats are shorter in summer. This keeps the goats cool.

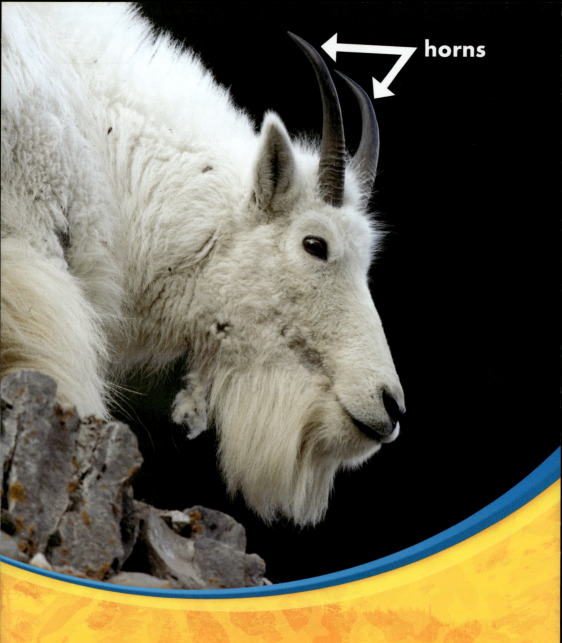

horns

Mountain goats have two horns. Their horns are black and **curved**.

These goats may use their horns to fight.

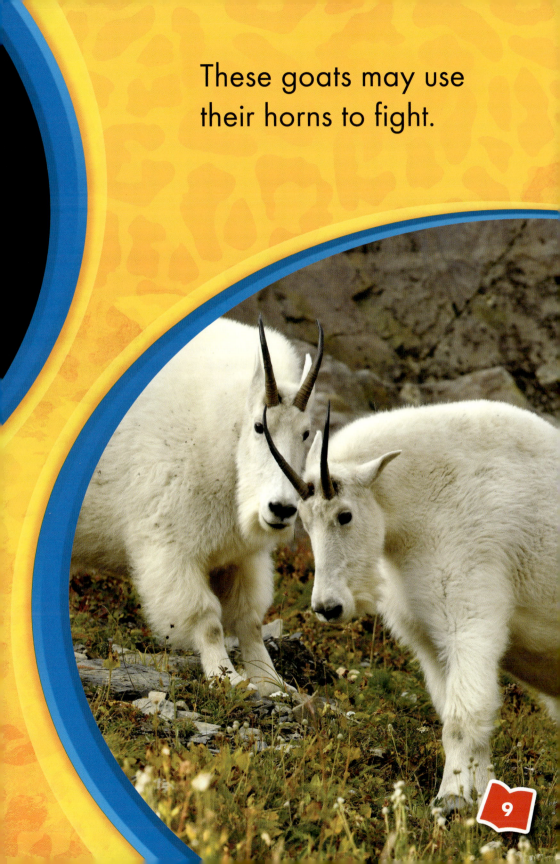

Mountain goats have strong legs and wide **hooves**. These help the goats climb.

Their hooves have pads on the bottom. These pads **grip** rocky, snowy areas.

hooves

Strong Climbers!

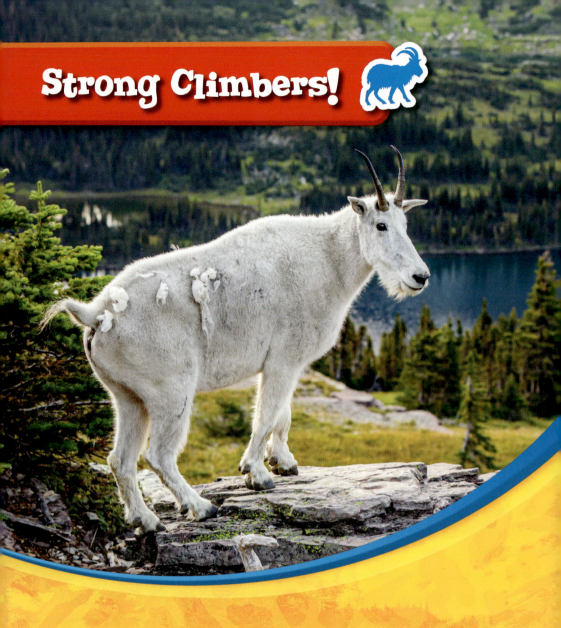

These goats mostly live on mountains. Some move to forests in winter.

Nannies live together with their young. **Billies** often live alone.

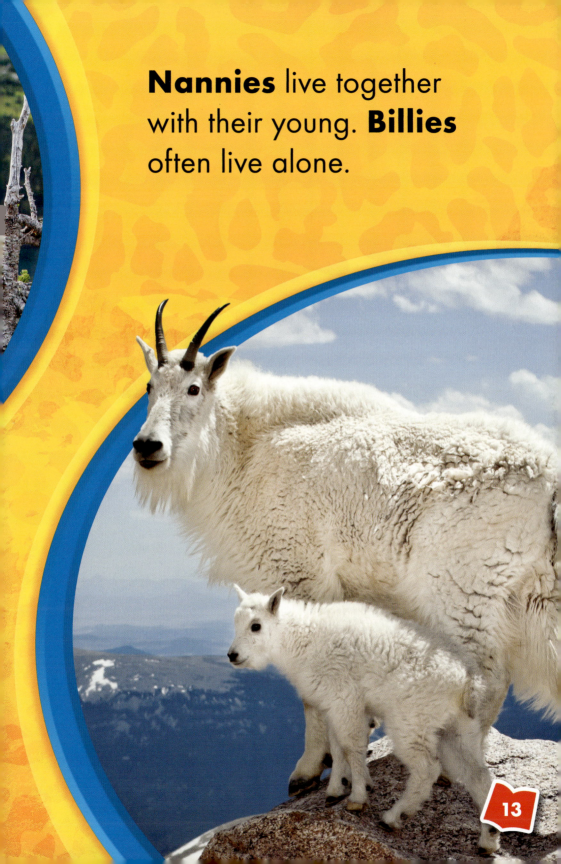

Mountain goats are strong climbers! They easily climb where other animals cannot.

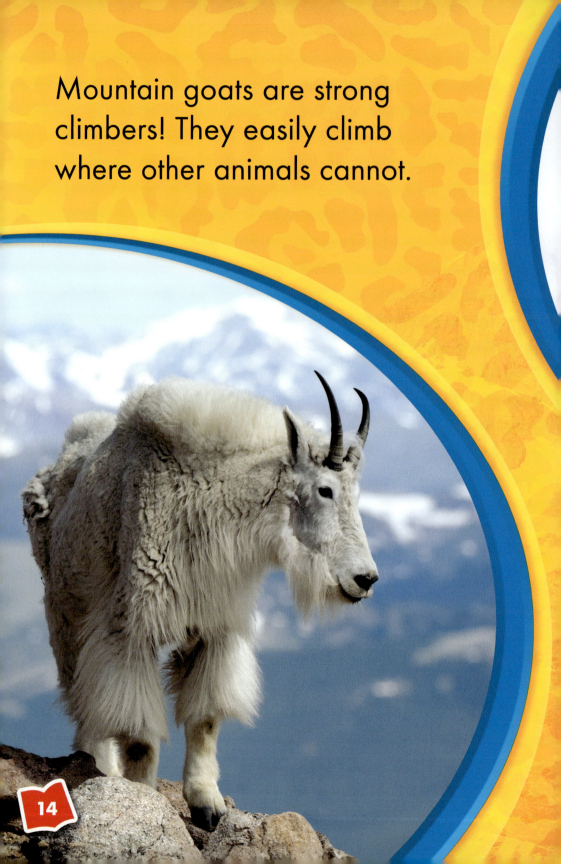

cougar

High cliffs keep them safe from **predators**. Their main predators are cougars and wolves.

Mountain goats are **herbivores**. They mostly eat grasses and mosses.

They may lick rocks to get **minerals**. The minerals help them regrow their coats.

Growing Up

Nannies usually give birth to one **kid** at a time. Minutes after birth, kids stand up.

After about one week, kids join a **nursery**.

kid

nursery

Kids stay close to mom. She keeps them safe from harm.

After about one year, kids live on their own. They can live up to 18 years!

Life of a Mountain Goat

Name of Babies
kids

Number of Babies
1

Time Spent with Mom
about 1 year

Life Span
up to 18 years

Glossary

billies—male mountain goats

cliffs—high, steep surfaces of rock, earth, or ice

coats—the fur or hair covering some animals

curved—having a hook

grip—to hold tightly

herbivores—animals that only eat plants

hooves—hard coverings on the feet of some animals

kid—a baby mountain goat

mammals—warm-blooded animals that have backbones and feed their young milk

minerals—elements found in the earth that are needed to stay healthy

nannies—female mountain goats

nursery—a group of nannies and kids that live together

predators—animals that hunt other animals for food

shaggy—having long, rough hair

To Learn More

AT THE LIBRARY

Davidson, Rose. *Goats*. Washington, D.C.: National Geographic, 2023.

Neuenfeldt, Elizabeth. *Mountain Animals*. Minneapolis, Minn.: Bellwether Media, 2023.

Shaffer, Lindsay. *Mountain Goats*. Minneapolis, Minn.: Bellwether Media, 2020.

ON THE WEB

Factsurfer.com gives you a safe, fun way to find more information.

1. Go to www.factsurfer.com.

2. Enter "mountain goats" into the search box and click 🔍.

3. Select your book cover to see a list of related content.

23

Index

billies, 13
cliffs, 4, 15
climb, 4, 10, 14
coats, 6, 7, 17
colors, 6, 8
fight, 9
food, 16, 17
forests, 12
herbivores, 16
hooves, 10
horns, 8, 9
kid, 18, 20, 21
legs, 10
life of a mountain goat, 21
mammals, 4
minerals, 17
mom, 20
mountains, 12

nannies, 13, 18
North America, 4
nursery, 18, 19
pads, 10
predators, 15
range, 4, 5
spot a mountain goat, 11
status, 5
summer, 7
winter, 6, 12

The images in this book are reproduced through the courtesy of: Robert Harding Video, cover (mountain goat); Alexey Kamenskiy, cover background, interior background; adipra52, cover (mountain goat icon); Jenny CC Carter, p. 3; Diane Garcia, p. 4; Ronnie Howard, p. 6; Jessica Lichon, p. 7; moosehenderson, p. 8; mlharing, p. 9; Nina, pp. 10, 21; JackF, p. 11; jaypetersen, pp. 10-11; Diane, p. 12; joshschutz, p. 13; Chris Rubino, p. 14; moodboard, p. 15; YellowDoorProductions, pp. 16-17; Chris, p. 17 (cougars); christopher, p. 17 (mosses); Piotr Krzeslak, p. 17 (brown bears); Andrew_Swarga, p. 17 (grasses); Karel Bartik, p. 17 (wolves); Scalia Media, p. 17 (mountain goat); Jaynes Gallery/ Danita Delimont, p. 18; Druce Montagne/ Dembinsky Photo Associates/ Alamy, pp. 18-19; Paul Tessier, p. 20; Paul, p. 23.

24